50 Premium International Japanese Pizza Dishes

By: Kelly Johnson

Table of Contents

- Okonomiyaki Pizza
- Teriyaki Chicken Pizza
- Shrimp Tempura Pizza
- Ebi Mayo (Shrimp Mayonnaise) Pizza
- Tonkatsu Pizza
- Unagi (Grilled Eel) Pizza
- Miso Beef Pizza
- Kimchi and Pork Pizza
- Wasabi Chicken Pizza
- Spicy Tuna Pizza
- Salmon Roe and Avocado Pizza
- Japanese Curry Pizza
- Tofu and Veggie Pizza
- Shoyu Chicken Pizza
- Yakiniku Beef Pizza
- Katsu-Curry Pizza
- Japanese Bacon and Egg Pizza
- Teriyaki Salmon Pizza
- Sukiyaki Beef Pizza
- Mushroom and Soy Sauce Pizza
- Seaweed and Sesame Pizza
- Okonomiyaki-style Pizza with Mayonnaise
- Sweet Potato and Miso Pizza
- Japanese Hot Pot Pizza
- Grilled Scallop Pizza
- Spicy Udon Noodle Pizza
- Japanese Cheese Pizza with Soy Sauce
- Sake Salmon and Cream Cheese Pizza
- Matcha and Chocolate Pizza
- Gyoza Pizza
- Tempura Vegetables Pizza
- Shiso Leaf and Mozzarella Pizza
- Japanese Pickled Plum (Ume) Pizza
- Japanese Sweet Corn and Bacon Pizza
- Mentaiko (Spicy Cod Roe) Pizza

- Japanese Spicy Chicken Pizza
- Yuzu and Tofu Pizza
- Sukiyaki-style Pizza
- Ramen Pizza
- Miso-Glazed Salmon Pizza
- Okonomiyaki-inspired Seafood Pizza
- Wasabi and Avocado Pizza
- Tofu and Seaweed Pizza
- Grilled Pork and Apple Pizza
- Japanese-style Margherita Pizza
- Spicy Miso Ramen Pizza
- Japanese Prawn and Avocado Pizza
- Kabocha (Pumpkin) and Cheese Pizza
- Roasted Garlic and Miso Pizza
- Tamago (Japanese Omelette) Pizza

Okonomiyaki Pizza

Ingredients:

- 1 pizza dough
- 1/4 cup okonomiyaki sauce
- 1/2 cup shredded mozzarella cheese
- 1/4 cup cabbage, finely shredded
- 1/4 cup cooked bacon, chopped
- 1 egg
- Bonito flakes (optional)
- Kewpie mayonnaise for drizzling
- Green onions for garnish

Instructions:

1. Preheat oven to 475°F (245°C).
2. Roll out the pizza dough and brush with okonomiyaki sauce.
3. Top with mozzarella cheese, shredded cabbage, cooked bacon, and crack the egg on top.
4. Bake for 10-12 minutes, until the crust is golden and the egg is cooked.
5. Drizzle with kewpie mayonnaise and sprinkle with bonito flakes and green onions before serving.

Teriyaki Chicken Pizza

Ingredients:

- 1 pizza dough
- 1/4 cup teriyaki sauce
- 1/2 cup shredded mozzarella cheese
- 1/2 cup cooked chicken, shredded
- 1/4 cup red onion, thinly sliced
- 1/4 cup green bell pepper, sliced
- Fresh cilantro for garnish

Instructions:

1. Preheat oven to 475°F (245°C).
2. Roll out the pizza dough and brush with teriyaki sauce.
3. Top with mozzarella cheese, shredded chicken, red onion, and green bell pepper.
4. Bake for 10-12 minutes, until the crust is golden and the cheese is melted.
5. Garnish with fresh cilantro before serving.

Shrimp Tempura Pizza

Ingredients:

- 1 pizza dough
- 1/4 cup soy sauce
- 1/2 cup mozzarella cheese
- 6-8 shrimp tempura, chopped
- 1/4 cup green onions, sliced
- Kewpie mayonnaise for drizzling

Instructions:

1. Preheat oven to 475°F (245°C).
2. Roll out the pizza dough and brush with soy sauce.
3. Top with mozzarella cheese and chopped shrimp tempura.
4. Bake for 10-12 minutes, until the crust is golden and the cheese is melted.
5. Drizzle with kewpie mayonnaise and garnish with sliced green onions before serving.

Ebi Mayo (Shrimp Mayonnaise) Pizza

Ingredients:

- 1 pizza dough
- 1/4 cup teriyaki sauce
- 1/2 cup mozzarella cheese
- 1/2 cup cooked shrimp, peeled and deveined
- 2 tbsp mayonnaise
- 1 tsp sriracha sauce (optional)
- Fresh cilantro for garnish

Instructions:

1. Preheat oven to 475°F (245°C).
2. Roll out the pizza dough and brush with teriyaki sauce.
3. Top with mozzarella cheese and cooked shrimp.
4. Bake for 10-12 minutes, until the crust is golden and the cheese is melted.
5. Mix mayonnaise with sriracha (if using), drizzle over the pizza, and garnish with fresh cilantro before serving.

Tonkatsu Pizza

Ingredients:

- 1 pizza dough
- 1/4 cup tonkatsu sauce
- 1/2 cup mozzarella cheese
- 1/4 cup cooked pork cutlet, sliced
- 1/4 cup shredded cabbage
- Pickled ginger for garnish

Instructions:

1. Preheat oven to 475°F (245°C).
2. Roll out the pizza dough and brush with tonkatsu sauce.
3. Top with mozzarella cheese, sliced pork cutlet, and shredded cabbage.
4. Bake for 10-12 minutes, until the crust is golden and the cheese is melted.
5. Garnish with pickled ginger before serving.

Unagi (Grilled Eel) Pizza

Ingredients:

- 1 pizza dough
- 1/4 cup eel sauce
- 1/2 cup mozzarella cheese
- 1/4 cup grilled eel (unagi), sliced
- 1/4 cup cucumber, thinly sliced
- Fresh sesame seeds for garnish

Instructions:

1. Preheat oven to 475°F (245°C).
2. Roll out the pizza dough and brush with eel sauce.
3. Top with mozzarella cheese and grilled eel slices.
4. Bake for 10-12 minutes, until the crust is golden and the cheese is melted.
5. Garnish with thin cucumber slices and sesame seeds before serving.

Miso Beef Pizza

Ingredients:

- 1 pizza dough
- 1/4 cup miso paste
- 1/2 cup shredded mozzarella cheese
- 1/4 cup cooked ground beef
- 1/4 cup mushrooms, sliced
- Fresh green onions for garnish

Instructions:

1. Preheat oven to 475°F (245°C).
2. Roll out the pizza dough and spread a thin layer of miso paste.
3. Top with mozzarella cheese, cooked ground beef, and sliced mushrooms.
4. Bake for 10-12 minutes, until the crust is golden and the cheese is melted.
5. Garnish with fresh green onions before serving.

Kimchi and Pork Pizza

Ingredients:

- 1 pizza dough
- 1/4 cup gochujang sauce
- 1/2 cup shredded mozzarella cheese
- 1/4 cup kimchi, chopped
- 1/4 cup cooked pork, shredded
- Fresh cilantro for garnish

Instructions:

1. Preheat oven to 475°F (245°C).
2. Roll out the pizza dough and spread a thin layer of gochujang sauce.
3. Top with mozzarella cheese, chopped kimchi, and shredded cooked pork.
4. Bake for 10-12 minutes, until the crust is golden and the cheese is melted.
5. Garnish with fresh cilantro before serving.

Wasabi Chicken Pizza

Ingredients:

- 1 pizza dough
- 1/4 cup wasabi mayo
- 1/2 cup shredded mozzarella cheese
- 1/4 cup cooked chicken, shredded
- 1/4 cup red onion, thinly sliced
- Fresh cilantro for garnish

Instructions:

1. Preheat oven to 475°F (245°C).
2. Roll out the pizza dough and spread wasabi mayo evenly.
3. Top with mozzarella cheese, shredded chicken, and sliced red onion.
4. Bake for 10-12 minutes, until the crust is golden and the cheese is melted.
5. Garnish with fresh cilantro before serving.

Spicy Tuna Pizza

Ingredients:

- 1 pizza dough
- 1/4 cup spicy mayo
- 1/2 cup shredded mozzarella cheese
- 1/4 cup sushi-grade tuna, diced
- 1/4 cup cucumber, thinly sliced
- Fresh sesame seeds for garnish

Instructions:

1. Preheat oven to 475°F (245°C).
2. Roll out the pizza dough and spread spicy mayo evenly.
3. Top with mozzarella cheese and diced sushi-grade tuna.
4. Bake for 10-12 minutes, until the crust is golden and the cheese is melted.
5. Garnish with cucumber slices and sesame seeds before serving.

Salmon Roe and Avocado Pizza

Ingredients:

- 1 pizza dough
- 1/4 cup wasabi mayo
- 1/2 cup shredded mozzarella cheese
- 1/4 cup sliced avocado
- 2 tbsp salmon roe
- Fresh cilantro for garnish
- Lemon wedges for serving

Instructions:

1. Preheat oven to 475°F (245°C).
2. Roll out the pizza dough and spread wasabi mayo evenly.
3. Top with mozzarella cheese and bake for 10-12 minutes, until the crust is golden and the cheese is melted.
4. Once out of the oven, top with sliced avocado, salmon roe, and fresh cilantro.
5. Serve with lemon wedges.

Japanese Curry Pizza

Ingredients:

- 1 pizza dough
- 1/4 cup Japanese curry sauce
- 1/2 cup shredded mozzarella cheese
- 1/4 cup cooked chicken or beef, shredded
- 1/4 cup onions, thinly sliced
- 1/4 cup carrots, diced
- Fresh cilantro for garnish

Instructions:

1. Preheat oven to 475°F (245°C).
2. Roll out the pizza dough and spread a thin layer of Japanese curry sauce.
3. Top with mozzarella cheese, cooked chicken or beef, onions, and diced carrots.
4. Bake for 10-12 minutes, until the crust is golden and the cheese is melted.
5. Garnish with fresh cilantro before serving.

Tofu and Veggie Pizza

Ingredients:

- 1 pizza dough
- 1/4 cup hoisin sauce
- 1/2 cup shredded mozzarella cheese
- 1/4 cup tofu, cubed
- 1/4 cup bell peppers, sliced
- 1/4 cup mushrooms, sliced
- Fresh cilantro for garnish

Instructions:

1. Preheat oven to 475°F (245°C).
2. Roll out the pizza dough and spread hoisin sauce evenly.
3. Top with mozzarella cheese, tofu, bell peppers, and mushrooms.
4. Bake for 10-12 minutes, until the crust is golden and the cheese is melted.
5. Garnish with fresh cilantro before serving.

Shoyu Chicken Pizza

Ingredients:

- 1 pizza dough
- 1/4 cup shoyu sauce (soy sauce)
- 1/2 cup shredded mozzarella cheese
- 1/4 cup cooked chicken, shredded
- 1/4 cup onions, thinly sliced
- 1/4 cup green onions, sliced
- Sesame seeds for garnish

Instructions:

1. Preheat oven to 475°F (245°C).
2. Roll out the pizza dough and brush with shoyu sauce.
3. Top with mozzarella cheese, shredded chicken, onions, and green onions.
4. Bake for 10-12 minutes, until the crust is golden and the cheese is melted.
5. Garnish with sesame seeds before serving.

Yakiniku Beef Pizza

Ingredients:

- 1 pizza dough
- 1/4 cup yakiniku sauce
- 1/2 cup shredded mozzarella cheese
- 1/4 cup cooked yakiniku beef, thinly sliced
- 1/4 cup onions, thinly sliced
- Fresh green onions for garnish

Instructions:

1. Preheat oven to 475°F (245°C).
2. Roll out the pizza dough and brush with yakiniku sauce.
3. Top with mozzarella cheese, yakiniku beef, and onions.
4. Bake for 10-12 minutes, until the crust is golden and the cheese is melted.
5. Garnish with fresh green onions before serving.

Katsu-Curry Pizza

Ingredients:

- 1 pizza dough
- 1/4 cup katsu curry sauce
- 1/2 cup shredded mozzarella cheese
- 1/4 cup cooked pork cutlet, sliced
- 1/4 cup onions, thinly sliced
- Fresh parsley for garnish

Instructions:

1. Preheat oven to 475°F (245°C).
2. Roll out the pizza dough and spread a thin layer of katsu curry sauce.
3. Top with mozzarella cheese, sliced pork cutlet, and onions.
4. Bake for 10-12 minutes, until the crust is golden and the cheese is melted.
5. Garnish with fresh parsley before serving.

Japanese Bacon and Egg Pizza

Ingredients:

- 1 pizza dough
- 1/4 cup soy sauce
- 1/2 cup shredded mozzarella cheese
- 1/4 cup cooked bacon, chopped
- 1 egg
- Green onions for garnish

Instructions:

1. Preheat oven to 475°F (245°C).
2. Roll out the pizza dough and brush with soy sauce.
3. Top with mozzarella cheese and chopped bacon.
4. Crack an egg onto the pizza and bake for 10-12 minutes, until the crust is golden and the egg is cooked.
5. Garnish with green onions before serving.

Teriyaki Salmon Pizza

Ingredients:

- 1 pizza dough
- 1/4 cup teriyaki sauce
- 1/2 cup shredded mozzarella cheese
- 1/4 cup cooked salmon, flaked
- 1/4 cup red onions, thinly sliced
- Fresh cilantro for garnish

Instructions:

1. Preheat oven to 475°F (245°C).
2. Roll out the pizza dough and brush with teriyaki sauce.
3. Top with mozzarella cheese, flaked salmon, and red onions.
4. Bake for 10-12 minutes, until the crust is golden and the cheese is melted.
5. Garnish with fresh cilantro before serving.

Sukiyaki Beef Pizza

Ingredients:

- 1 pizza dough
- 1/4 cup sukiyaki sauce
- 1/2 cup shredded mozzarella cheese
- 1/4 cup cooked sukiyaki beef, thinly sliced
- 1/4 cup onions, thinly sliced
- Fresh green onions for garnish

Instructions:

1. Preheat oven to 475°F (245°C).
2. Roll out the pizza dough and brush with sukiyaki sauce.
3. Top with mozzarella cheese, sukiyaki beef, and onions.
4. Bake for 10-12 minutes, until the crust is golden and the cheese is melted.
5. Garnish with fresh green onions before serving.

Mushroom and Soy Sauce Pizza

Ingredients:

- 1 pizza dough
- 1/4 cup soy sauce
- 1/2 cup shredded mozzarella cheese
- 1/4 cup mushrooms, sliced
- 1/4 cup green onions, sliced
- Fresh sesame seeds for garnish

Instructions:

1. Preheat oven to 475°F (245°C).
2. Roll out the pizza dough and brush with soy sauce.
3. Top with mozzarella cheese, sliced mushrooms, and green onions.
4. Bake for 10-12 minutes, until the crust is golden and the cheese is melted.
5. Garnish with sesame seeds before serving.

Seaweed and Sesame Pizza

Ingredients:

- 1 pizza dough
- 1/4 cup soy sauce
- 1/2 cup shredded mozzarella cheese
- 1/4 cup seaweed (nori) strips
- 1/4 cup sesame seeds
- Green onions for garnish

Instructions:

1. Preheat oven to 475°F (245°C).
2. Roll out the pizza dough and brush with soy sauce.
3. Top with mozzarella cheese and bake for 10-12 minutes, until the crust is golden and the cheese is melted.
4. Once out of the oven, sprinkle with seaweed strips, sesame seeds, and green onions before serving.

Okonomiyaki-style Pizza with Mayonnaise

Ingredients:

- 1 pizza dough
- 1/4 cup okonomiyaki sauce
- 1/2 cup shredded mozzarella cheese
- 1/4 cup cabbage, shredded
- 1/4 cup cooked pork belly or bacon, sliced
- 1/4 cup green onions, sliced
- Japanese mayonnaise for drizzling
- Bonito flakes for garnish

Instructions:

1. Preheat oven to 475°F (245°C).
2. Roll out the pizza dough and spread okonomiyaki sauce evenly.
3. Top with mozzarella cheese, shredded cabbage, and cooked pork belly or bacon.
4. Bake for 10-12 minutes, until the crust is golden and the cheese is melted.
5. Drizzle with Japanese mayonnaise and garnish with green onions and bonito flakes before serving.

Sweet Potato and Miso Pizza

Ingredients:

- 1 pizza dough
- 2 tbsp miso paste
- 1/2 cup shredded mozzarella cheese
- 1 small sweet potato, thinly sliced
- 1/4 cup red onions, thinly sliced
- Fresh cilantro for garnish

Instructions:

1. Preheat oven to 475°F (245°C).
2. Mix miso paste with a little water to thin it out and spread it over the pizza dough.
3. Top with mozzarella cheese, sweet potato slices, and red onions.
4. Bake for 12-15 minutes, until the crust is golden and the sweet potatoes are tender.
5. Garnish with fresh cilantro before serving.

Japanese Hot Pot Pizza

Ingredients:

- 1 pizza dough
- 1/4 cup soy sauce
- 1/2 cup shredded mozzarella cheese
- 1/4 cup shiitake mushrooms, sliced
- 1/4 cup tofu, cubed
- 1/4 cup napa cabbage, chopped
- 1/4 cup green onions, sliced
- 1 egg (optional, for cracking on top)

Instructions:

1. Preheat oven to 475°F (245°C).
2. Brush the pizza dough with soy sauce.
3. Top with mozzarella cheese, shiitake mushrooms, tofu, napa cabbage, and green onions.
4. If desired, crack an egg in the center of the pizza.
5. Bake for 10-12 minutes, until the crust is golden and the egg is cooked.

Grilled Scallop Pizza

Ingredients:

- 1 pizza dough
- 1/4 cup garlic butter
- 1/2 cup shredded mozzarella cheese
- 8-10 scallops, grilled and sliced
- 1/4 cup spinach, wilted
- Fresh lemon zest for garnish

Instructions:

1. Preheat oven to 475°F (245°C).
2. Roll out the pizza dough and brush with garlic butter.
3. Top with mozzarella cheese, grilled scallops, and wilted spinach.
4. Bake for 10-12 minutes, until the crust is golden and the cheese is melted.
5. Garnish with lemon zest before serving.

Spicy Udon Noodle Pizza

Ingredients:

- 1 pizza dough
- 1/4 cup spicy sesame paste or sriracha mayo
- 1/2 cup shredded mozzarella cheese
- 1/4 cup cooked udon noodles, drained
- 1/4 cup red onions, thinly sliced
- 1/4 cup cucumber, julienned
- Fresh cilantro for garnish

Instructions:

1. Preheat oven to 475°F (245°C).
2. Roll out the pizza dough and spread spicy sesame paste or sriracha mayo evenly.
3. Top with mozzarella cheese, cooked udon noodles, red onions, and cucumber.
4. Bake for 10-12 minutes, until the crust is golden and the cheese is melted.
5. Garnish with fresh cilantro before serving.

Japanese Cheese Pizza with Soy Sauce

Ingredients:

- 1 pizza dough
- 1 tbsp soy sauce
- 1/2 cup shredded mozzarella cheese
- 1/4 cup shredded cheddar cheese
- 1/4 cup parmesan cheese
- Fresh basil for garnish

Instructions:

1. Preheat oven to 475°F (245°C).
2. Roll out the pizza dough and brush with soy sauce.
3. Top with mozzarella cheese, cheddar cheese, and parmesan cheese.
4. Bake for 10-12 minutes, until the crust is golden and the cheese is melted.
5. Garnish with fresh basil before serving.

Sake Salmon and Cream Cheese Pizza

Ingredients:

- 1 pizza dough
- 1 tbsp soy sauce
- 1/4 cup cream cheese, softened
- 1/2 cup shredded mozzarella cheese
- 4 oz smoked salmon, thinly sliced
- 1/4 cup green onions, sliced
- Fresh dill for garnish

Instructions:

1. Preheat oven to 475°F (245°C).
2. Roll out the pizza dough and brush with soy sauce.
3. Spread a thin layer of cream cheese on the dough.
4. Top with mozzarella cheese, smoked salmon, and green onions.
5. Bake for 10-12 minutes, until the crust is golden and the cheese is melted.
6. Garnish with fresh dill before serving.

Matcha and Chocolate Pizza

Ingredients:

- 1 pizza dough
- 2 tbsp matcha powder
- 1/4 cup white chocolate chips
- 1/4 cup dark chocolate chips
- 1/4 cup crushed almonds (optional)
- Powdered sugar for dusting

Instructions:

1. Preheat oven to 475°F (245°C).
2. Roll out the pizza dough and brush with a little butter.
3. Sprinkle matcha powder over the dough, then top with white chocolate chips, dark chocolate chips, and crushed almonds.
4. Bake for 8-10 minutes, until the crust is golden and the chocolate has melted.
5. Dust with powdered sugar before serving.

Gyoza Pizza

Ingredients:

- 1 pizza dough
- 1/4 cup hoisin sauce
- 1/2 cup shredded mozzarella cheese
- 1/4 cup cooked ground pork or chicken
- 1/4 cup cabbage, shredded
- 1/4 cup green onions, sliced
- Fresh cilantro for garnish

Instructions:

1. Preheat oven to 475°F (245°C).
2. Roll out the pizza dough and spread hoisin sauce evenly.
3. Top with mozzarella cheese, cooked ground pork or chicken, shredded cabbage, and green onions.
4. Bake for 10-12 minutes, until the crust is golden and the cheese is melted.
5. Garnish with fresh cilantro before serving.

Tempura Vegetables Pizza

Ingredients:

- 1 pizza dough
- 1/4 cup tempura batter (prepared)
- 1/2 cup shredded mozzarella cheese
- 1/4 cup tempura-fried vegetables (sweet potato, zucchini, mushrooms)
- Soy dipping sauce for drizzling

Instructions:

1. Preheat oven to 475°F (245°C).
2. Roll out the pizza dough and top with shredded mozzarella cheese.
3. Fry tempura vegetables in batter according to package instructions, and arrange them on top of the pizza.
4. Bake for 10-12 minutes, until the crust is golden and the cheese is melted.
5. Drizzle with soy dipping sauce before serving.

Shiso Leaf and Mozzarella Pizza

Ingredients:

- 1 pizza dough
- 1/4 cup olive oil
- 1/2 cup shredded mozzarella cheese
- 1/4 cup fresh shiso leaves, chopped
- 1/4 cup red onions, thinly sliced
- Fresh sesame seeds for garnish

Instructions:

1. Preheat oven to 475°F (245°C).
2. Roll out the pizza dough and brush with olive oil.
3. Top with mozzarella cheese, chopped shiso leaves, and red onions.
4. Bake for 10-12 minutes, until the crust is golden and the cheese is melted.
5. Garnish with sesame seeds before serving.

Japanese Pickled Plum (Ume) Pizza

Ingredients:

- 1 pizza dough
- 2 tbsp umeboshi (pickled plum paste)
- 1/2 cup shredded mozzarella cheese
- 1/4 cup cooked chicken or pork, thinly sliced
- 1/4 cup fresh spinach
- 1 tbsp sesame seeds

Instructions:

1. Preheat oven to 475°F (245°C).
2. Spread umeboshi paste evenly over the pizza dough.
3. Top with mozzarella cheese, cooked chicken or pork, and spinach.
4. Bake for 10-12 minutes, until the crust is golden and the cheese is melted.
5. Garnish with sesame seeds before serving.

Japanese Sweet Corn and Bacon Pizza

Ingredients:

- 1 pizza dough
- 2 tbsp soy sauce
- 1/2 cup shredded mozzarella cheese
- 1/4 cup sweet corn kernels
- 1/4 cup cooked bacon, crumbled
- 1/4 cup green onions, chopped

Instructions:

1. Preheat oven to 475°F (245°C).
2. Brush the pizza dough with soy sauce.
3. Top with mozzarella cheese, sweet corn, cooked bacon, and green onions.
4. Bake for 10-12 minutes, until the crust is golden and the cheese is melted.
5. Serve hot with a sprinkle of additional green onions.

Mentaiko (Spicy Cod Roe) Pizza

Ingredients:

- 1 pizza dough
- 2 tbsp mentaiko (spicy cod roe)
- 1/2 cup shredded mozzarella cheese
- 1/4 cup cooked shrimp, chopped
- 1/4 cup sliced scallions
- A drizzle of mayonnaise

Instructions:

1. Preheat oven to 475°F (245°C).
2. Spread mentaiko evenly on the pizza dough.
3. Top with mozzarella cheese, chopped shrimp, and sliced scallions.
4. Bake for 10-12 minutes, until the crust is golden and the cheese is melted.
5. Drizzle with mayonnaise before serving.

Japanese Spicy Chicken Pizza

Ingredients:

- 1 pizza dough
- 2 tbsp spicy miso paste
- 1/2 cup shredded mozzarella cheese
- 1/4 cup cooked chicken, shredded
- 1/4 cup red onions, thinly sliced
- 1 tbsp sesame seeds

Instructions:

1. Preheat oven to 475°F (245°C).
2. Spread spicy miso paste over the pizza dough.
3. Top with mozzarella cheese, shredded chicken, and red onions.
4. Bake for 10-12 minutes, until the crust is golden and the cheese is melted.
5. Garnish with sesame seeds before serving.

Yuzu and Tofu Pizza

Ingredients:

- 1 pizza dough
- 2 tbsp yuzu kosho (yuzu citrus paste)
- 1/2 cup shredded mozzarella cheese
- 1/4 cup firm tofu, crumbled
- 1/4 cup spinach, chopped
- A drizzle of sesame oil

Instructions:

1. Preheat oven to 475°F (245°C).
2. Spread yuzu kosho over the pizza dough.
3. Top with mozzarella cheese, crumbled tofu, and chopped spinach.
4. Bake for 10-12 minutes, until the crust is golden and the cheese is melted.
5. Drizzle with sesame oil before serving.

Sukiyaki-style Pizza

Ingredients:

- 1 pizza dough
- 1/4 cup sukiyaki sauce
- 1/2 cup shredded mozzarella cheese
- 1/4 cup cooked beef, thinly sliced
- 1/4 cup onions, thinly sliced
- 1/4 cup shiitake mushrooms, sliced

Instructions:

1. Preheat oven to 475°F (245°C).
2. Brush the pizza dough with sukiyaki sauce.
3. Top with mozzarella cheese, cooked beef, onions, and shiitake mushrooms.
4. Bake for 10-12 minutes, until the crust is golden and the cheese is melted.

Ramen Pizza

Ingredients:

- 1 pizza dough
- 2 tbsp soy sauce
- 1/2 cup shredded mozzarella cheese
- 1/4 cup cooked ramen noodles, drained
- 1/4 cup cooked pork belly, sliced
- 1/4 cup green onions, chopped

Instructions:

1. Preheat oven to 475°F (245°C).
2. Spread soy sauce over the pizza dough.
3. Top with mozzarella cheese, cooked ramen noodles, sliced pork belly, and green onions.
4. Bake for 10-12 minutes, until the crust is golden and the cheese is melted.
5. Serve with additional soy sauce for dipping.

Miso-Glazed Salmon Pizza

Ingredients:

- 1 pizza dough
- 2 tbsp miso glaze
- 1/2 cup shredded mozzarella cheese
- 1/4 cup cooked salmon, flaked
- 1/4 cup spinach, chopped
- 1/4 cup sesame seeds

Instructions:

1. Preheat oven to 475°F (245°C).
2. Brush miso glaze evenly over the pizza dough.
3. Top with mozzarella cheese, flaked salmon, chopped spinach, and sesame seeds.
4. Bake for 10-12 minutes, until the crust is golden and the cheese is melted.
5. Garnish with additional sesame seeds before serving.

Okonomiyaki-inspired Seafood Pizza

Ingredients:

- 1 pizza dough
- 2 tbsp okonomiyaki sauce
- 1/2 cup shredded mozzarella cheese
- 1/4 cup cooked shrimp, chopped
- 1/4 cup scallops, cooked and sliced
- 1/4 cup cabbage, shredded
- A drizzle of Japanese mayonnaise

Instructions:

1. Preheat oven to 475°F (245°C).
2. Spread okonomiyaki sauce evenly over the pizza dough.
3. Top with mozzarella cheese, shrimp, scallops, and shredded cabbage.
4. Bake for 10-12 minutes, until the crust is golden and the cheese is melted.
5. Drizzle with Japanese mayonnaise before serving.

Wasabi and Avocado Pizza

Ingredients:

- 1 pizza dough
- 2 tbsp wasabi paste
- 1/2 cup shredded mozzarella cheese
- 1/4 cup avocado, sliced
- 1/4 cup cooked shrimp, chopped
- 1 tbsp sesame seeds

Instructions:

1. Preheat oven to 475°F (245°C).
2. Spread wasabi paste evenly over the pizza dough.
3. Top with mozzarella cheese, sliced avocado, and chopped shrimp.
4. Bake for 10-12 minutes, until the crust is golden and the cheese is melted.
5. Garnish with sesame seeds before serving.

Tofu and Seaweed Pizza

Ingredients:

- 1 pizza dough
- 2 tbsp soy sauce
- 1/2 cup shredded mozzarella cheese
- 1/4 cup firm tofu, crumbled
- 1/4 cup nori (seaweed) strips
- 1/4 cup green onions, chopped
- A drizzle of sesame oil

Instructions:

1. Preheat oven to 475°F (245°C).
2. Brush the pizza dough with soy sauce.
3. Top with mozzarella cheese, crumbled tofu, nori strips, and chopped green onions.
4. Bake for 10-12 minutes, until the crust is golden and the cheese is melted.
5. Drizzle with sesame oil before serving.

Grilled Pork and Apple Pizza

Ingredients:

- 1 pizza dough
- 2 tbsp BBQ sauce
- 1/2 cup shredded mozzarella cheese
- 1/4 cup grilled pork, thinly sliced
- 1/4 cup thinly sliced apples
- 1/4 cup red onions, thinly sliced
- 1 tbsp fresh thyme leaves

Instructions:

1. Preheat oven to 475°F (245°C).
2. Brush the pizza dough with BBQ sauce.
3. Top with mozzarella cheese, grilled pork, sliced apples, red onions, and fresh thyme leaves.
4. Bake for 10-12 minutes, until the crust is golden and the cheese is melted.

Japanese-style Margherita Pizza

Ingredients:

- 1 pizza dough
- 1/4 cup tomato sauce
- 1/2 cup shredded mozzarella cheese
- 1/4 cup fresh basil leaves
- 1 tbsp yuzu zest
- A drizzle of sesame oil

Instructions:

1. Preheat oven to 475°F (245°C).
2. Spread tomato sauce evenly over the pizza dough.
3. Top with mozzarella cheese and fresh basil leaves.
4. Bake for 10-12 minutes, until the crust is golden and the cheese is melted.
5. Garnish with yuzu zest and a drizzle of sesame oil before serving.

Spicy Miso Ramen Pizza

Ingredients:

- 1 pizza dough
- 2 tbsp spicy miso paste
- 1/2 cup shredded mozzarella cheese
- 1/4 cup cooked ramen noodles, drained
- 1/4 cup cooked pork, thinly sliced
- 1/4 cup green onions, chopped

Instructions:

1. Preheat oven to 475°F (245°C).
2. Spread spicy miso paste evenly over the pizza dough.
3. Top with mozzarella cheese, ramen noodles, cooked pork, and chopped green onions.
4. Bake for 10-12 minutes, until the crust is golden and the cheese is melted.
5. Serve with extra miso paste or soy sauce if desired.

Japanese Prawn and Avocado Pizza

Ingredients:

- 1 pizza dough
- 2 tbsp soy sauce
- 1/2 cup shredded mozzarella cheese
- 1/4 cup cooked prawns, chopped
- 1/4 cup avocado, sliced
- 1 tbsp sesame seeds
- A drizzle of wasabi mayonnaise

Instructions:

1. Preheat oven to 475°F (245°C).
2. Brush the pizza dough with soy sauce.
3. Top with mozzarella cheese, chopped prawns, sliced avocado, and sesame seeds.
4. Bake for 10-12 minutes, until the crust is golden and the cheese is melted.
5. Drizzle with wasabi mayonnaise before serving.

Kabocha (Pumpkin) and Cheese Pizza

Ingredients:

- 1 pizza dough
- 1/2 cup kabocha pumpkin, roasted and mashed
- 1/2 cup shredded mozzarella cheese
- 1/4 cup crumbled feta cheese
- 1/4 cup fresh sage leaves, chopped
- A drizzle of olive oil

Instructions:

1. Preheat oven to 475°F (245°C).
2. Spread mashed kabocha pumpkin evenly over the pizza dough.
3. Top with mozzarella cheese, crumbled feta, and chopped fresh sage.
4. Bake for 10-12 minutes, until the crust is golden and the cheese is melted.
5. Drizzle with olive oil before serving.

Roasted Garlic and Miso Pizza

Ingredients:

- 1 pizza dough
- 2 tbsp white miso paste
- 1/2 cup shredded mozzarella cheese
- 1/4 cup roasted garlic, mashed
- 1/4 cup fresh parsley, chopped
- A drizzle of sesame oil

Instructions:

1. Preheat oven to 475°F (245°C).
2. Spread white miso paste evenly over the pizza dough.
3. Top with mozzarella cheese, roasted garlic, and fresh parsley.
4. Bake for 10-12 minutes, until the crust is golden and the cheese is melted.
5. Drizzle with sesame oil before serving.

Tamago (Japanese Omelette) Pizza

Ingredients:

- 1 pizza dough
- 2 tbsp soy sauce
- 1/2 cup shredded mozzarella cheese
- 2 large eggs, beaten and cooked into tamago (Japanese omelette)
- 1/4 cup green onions, chopped
- A drizzle of teriyaki sauce

Instructions:

1. Preheat oven to 475°F (245°C).
2. Brush the pizza dough with soy sauce.
3. Top with mozzarella cheese and cooked tamago (Japanese omelette) slices.
4. Bake for 10-12 minutes, until the crust is golden and the cheese is melted.
5. Garnish with chopped green onions and drizzle with teriyaki sauce before serving.

www.ingramcontent.com/pod-product-compliance
Lightning Source LLC
LaVergne TN
LVHW081500060526
838201LV00056BA/2854